ANIMAL MYTHS,
BUSTED!

by Jodie Mangor

www.12StoryLibrary.com

12-Story Library is an imprint of Peterson Publishing Company and Press Room Editions.

Produced for 12-Story Library by Red Line Editorial

Photographs ©: Baronb/Shutterstock Images, cover, 1, 20; Honey Clover/Shutterstock Images, 4; mountainpix/Shutterstock Images, 5, 26; Library of Congress, 6; J.N. Stuart/US Fish and Wildlife Service, 7; worldswildlifewonders/Shutterstock Images, 8; Susan Flashman/Shutterstock Images, 9; 1stGallery/Shutterstock Images, 10, 28; VGstockstudio/Shutterstock Images, 11; AndChisPhoto/Shutterstock Images, 12; Chantal de Bruijne/Shutterstock Images, 13; Anton_Ivanov/Shutterstock Images, 14; fullempty/Shutterstock Images, 15; Maxim Petrichuk/Shutterstock Images, 17; Ann Froschauer/US Fish and Wildlife Service, 18; Michael Lynch/Shutterstock Images, 19; curioustiger/iStockphoto, 21; Baishev/Shutterstock Images, 22, 29; Gil.K/Shutterstock Images, 23; Digital Vision./Photodisc/Thinkstock, 24; tratong/Shutterstock Images, 25; Alberto Loyo/Shutterstock Images, 27

Library of Congress Cataloging-in-Publication Data
Names: Mangor, Jodie, author.
Title: Animal myths, busted! / by Jodie Mangor.
Description: North Mankato, MN : 12-Story Library, [2017] | Series: Science
   myths, busted! | Includes bibliographical references and index.
Identifiers: LCCN 2016002360 (print) | LCCN 2016007046 (ebook) | ISBN
   9781632353009 (library bound : alk. paper) | ISBN 9781632353504 (pbk. :
   alk. paper) | ISBN 9781621434658 (hosted ebook)
Subjects: LCSH: Animals--Miscellanea--Juvenile literature.
Classification: LCC QL49 .M2135 2016 (print) | LCC QL49 (ebook) | DDC
   590.2--dc23
LC record available at http://lccn.loc.gov/2016002360

Printed in the United States of America
Mankato, MN
May, 2016

Access free, up-to-date content on this topic plus a full digital version of this book. Scan the QR code on page 31 or use your school's login at 12StoryLibrary.com.

Table of Contents

Hippos Sweat Blood 4

Birds Cannot Smell 6

Koalas Are Bears 8

Dogs Have Cleaner Mouths Than Humans Do 10

Cheetahs Overheat While Hunting 12

Ostriches Bury Their Heads in the Sand 14

Camels Store Water in Their Humps 16

Bats Are Blind 18

Sheep Are Not Very Bright 20

Chameleons Change Color to Blend In 22

Porcupines Shoot Their Quills 24

Snakes Unhinge Their Jaws to Swallow Prey 26

Fact Sheet 28

Glossary 30

For More Information 31

Index 32

About the Author 32

Busted:
Hippos Sweat Blood

Ancient Greeks were puzzled by the hippopotamus, or "hippo." The Greeks noticed hippo sweat looked red. The enormous African mammals seem to sweat blood. Nineteenth-century Europeans studied the phenomenon. Like the Greeks, the explorers assumed a hippo's sweat contained blood. They called the substance "blood sweat."

Scientists assumed the blood sweat protected the hippo's skin while in the water. This is true. But blood sweat is not sweat at all. Hippos do not have sweat glands. They are unable to sweat.

The blood sweat was not really blood either. Observers discovered

The red "blood sweat" of a hippo is not blood or sweat.

AGGRESSIVE PLANT EATERS

Hippos are usually slow-moving, plant-eating mammals. But if another animal threatens their territory, hippos will attack. They can move surprisingly fast, running up to 20 miles per hour (32 km/h). They can bite a crocodile in half. Hippos are considered the most dangerous mammal in Africa.

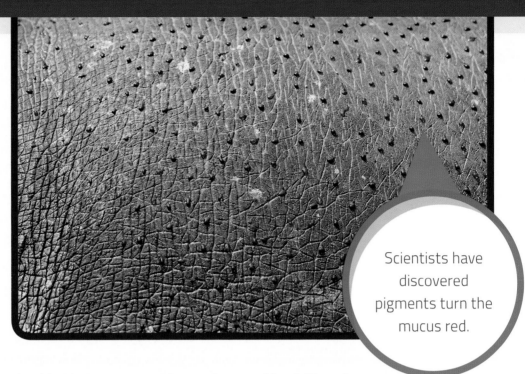

Scientists have discovered pigments turn the mucus red.

that blood sweat was really an oily mucus. It moisturizes the hippo's skin and protects it from the sun. The mucus makes the skin water repellant. It also protects hippos from germs in dirty, crowded watering holes. It protects them from infection if they are injured in a fight.

Exposure to sunlight turns the mucus red. It took until 2004 for scientists to discover what made so-called "blood sweat" red. Scientists in Japan studied the chemicals in blood sweat. They found there were two pigments in blood sweat. One is red, and one is orange. They help protect the hippo from getting sunburned. Hippos do not sweat blood. They do not sweat at all. Science helped bust an ancient myth.

6,460
Average weight, in pounds (2,930 kg), of an adult hippo.

- Scientists used to think hippo sweat had blood in it.
- Later, scientists discovered blood sweat is not sweat, but an oily mucus.
- The mucus turns red when exposed to sunlight.

Busted:
Birds Cannot Smell

The myth that birds cannot smell started in the 1820s. Renowned ornithologist John James Audubon was studying bird behavior. He theorized that vultures found dead animals to eat by sight, not smell. He wanted to test his idea.

First, Audubon stuffed a deerskin with grass. He put it in a meadow. It looked like a carcass but did not smell. A vulture flew down and tried to eat it. Then, Audubon hid a dead hog under some brush. It smelled of rotting meat but could not be seen. No vultures came. Audubon concluded that vultures do not use smell to find food. This is where the myth that birds cannot smell began.

Audubon's conclusion was considered truth for more than a century. But his methods were flawed. He did not distinguish between turkey vultures and black vultures. In 1927, ornithologist Frank Chapman studied both

THINK ABOUT IT

If you were going to test a bird's sense of smell, how would you do it?

Audubon devoted his life to studying birds.

Turkey vultures use their sense of smell when searching for food.

species. His research suggested turkey vultures hunted by smell. In 1960, ornithologist Kenneth Stager did some new experiments. He discovered turkey vultures do not like to eat very rotten meat. The hog Audubon used had been dead for days. Stager redid the experiment with fresher meat. Like Chapman, Stager found turkey vultures *do* use their sense of smell to find food. He even determined the specific chemical that attracts them.

Since then, scientists have tested many types of birds. They all react to odors. Today, scientists know birds use their sense of smell for many things. Odors can help them find food, mates, or their way home.

Birds do not have noses, but they do have nostrils. The part of their brain that senses smell is smaller than in other animals. Still, one thing is certain: Birds can sense a smell.

600
Number of smell-related genes found in kiwi and kakapos birds.

- For a long time, scientists have debated whether birds can smell.
- Vultures use odors to find food.
- Many bird behaviors are tied to their sense of smell.

Busted:
Koalas Are Bears

Europeans came to Australia in the late 1700s. They soon observed fuzzy, leaf-eating animals climbing in trees. The native aborigines called these animals koalas. But the animals reminded the Europeans of bears. They had round, furry ears and look cuddly. Around 1816, French naturalist Henri de Blainwill gave koalas their scientific name. He called them *Phascolarctos cinereus*. This means "ash-gray pouched bear" in Greek. This led many people to call koalas "koala bears."

But koalas are not bears. They are not even closely related to bears. Bears and koalas are both mammals. But that is where their similarities stop. Koalas are most similar to wombats. Both koalas and wombats are marsupials, a kind of mammal found mostly in Australia. Kangaroos are also marsupials.

Marsupials give birth to tiny babies. Newborn koalas are the size of a jellybean. They have no fur and cannot

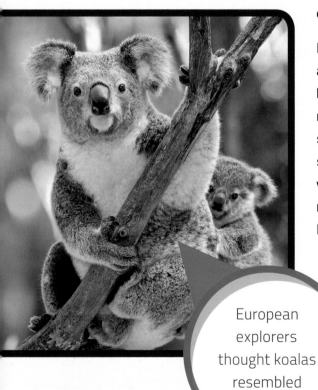

European explorers thought koalas resembled bears.

see. They nurse and grow inside a special pouch on the mother's body. Baby koalas spend approximately six months in this pouch. They stay with their mothers another six months after that.

Koala means "no drink" in a native Australian language. Many areas of Australia are very dry. Koalas rarely drink. They get most of their water from the eucalyptus leaves they eat. Many people think koalas will eat only eucalyptus leaves. But they have been known to eat leaves from some other types of trees, too.

18
Hours per day a koala sleeps.

- Koalas are marsupials, not bears.
- They carry their babies in pouches.
- They spend most of their time in eucalyptus trees.

A baby koala grows inside its mother's pouch for six months.

Busted: Dogs Have Cleaner Mouths Than Humans Do

Scientists used to think dogs' mouths were cleaner than humans' mouths. Dogs get fewer cavities than humans do. When dogs lick their wounds, the wounds heal quickly. Scientists have long thought human bites cause more serious infections than dog bites do.

But new studies show dog mouths are not clean. They have more bacteria in them than human mouths do. Dogs sometimes eat rotten food or other animals' feces. They will even use their tongues as toilet paper.

But there is some science behind the myth. Cavity-causing bacteria do not grow well in dogs' mouths. That is why dogs get fewer cavities than humans do. Cavity-causing bacteria eat the sugar on humans' teeth. The sugar comes from the food we eat.

Dog mouths contain more bacteria than human mouths do.

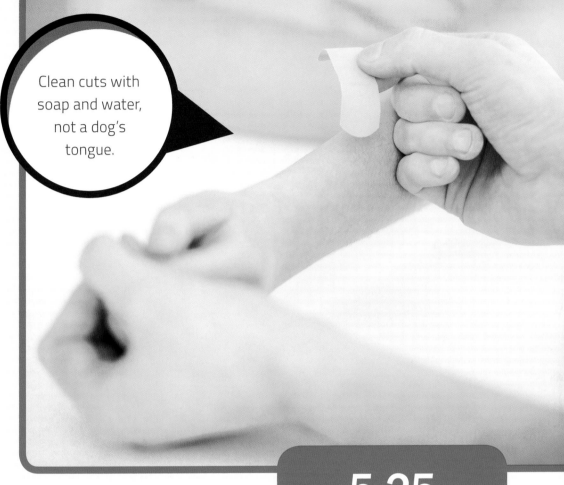

Clean cuts with soap and water, not a dog's tongue.

Dogs lick wounds to clear away dead tissue and dirt. Doctors clean people's wounds for the same reason. But they use tools instead of tongues. Cleaner wounds heal faster. Recent studies show most human bites are no worse than dog bites. The types of bacteria that live in human and dog mouths are different. Most dog germs are harmless to humans.

5.25
Percent of dogs with tooth decay.

- Dog mouths have more bacteria than human mouths do.
- Different bacteria are found in dog mouths compared with human mouths.
- Many of the bacteria in dog mouths are harmless to humans.

11

Busted: Cheetahs Overheat While Hunting

Cheetahs are the fastest land animals. They can reach speeds of 60 miles per hour (97 km/h) in 3 short seconds. Most cars cannot do that. Cheetahs chase their prey in short bursts. Many times, they give up on the chase. They catch fewer than one-half of the animals they hunt.

In 1973, scientists tested two captive cheetahs. They wanted to find out why cheetahs give up when

THINK ABOUT IT

Which results do you think are more true to life? The ones from the experiments done in 1973 or the ones from 2013? Why? Think of three ways new technologies make it easier for scientists to collect information.

chasing prey. The cheetahs ran on a treadmill at 12 miles per hour (30 km/h) for 1.2 miles (2 km). They

Cheetahs are quick and agile predators.

Cheetahs need to rest after an intense sprint.

stopped when their body temperature reached 104.9°F (40.5°C). The scientists concluded that cheetahs must give up their hunt when they get too hot. Soon, everyone believed this was true.

In 2013, a different group of scientists busted this myth. They studied wild cheetahs hunting in nature. The cheetahs ran 60 miles per hour (97 km/h) for short distances. Their body temperature did not go up when they ran. Instead, temperatures went up *after* the cheetahs stopped running. The cheetahs that caught prey had higher temperatures than the ones who did not.

These results have given scientists a new idea. Cheetahs have to guard their food from lions and hyenas. This could be stressful. Scientists believe stress is making the cheetahs' body temperature go up. But scientists are still trying to figure out why cheetahs give up on the chase so often.

22

Distance, in feet (6.7 m), a cheetah can cover in a single stride.

- Wild cheetahs do not overheat while hunting.
- Their body temperature goes up once they have caught something.
- Cheetahs have to protect their kills from other predators.

Busted: Ostriches Bury Their Heads in the Sand

The Roman naturalist Pliny the Elder lived around 70 CE. He observed that ostriches stick their heads in bushes. The ostriches think they are hidden. In time, Pliny's observation was reinterpreted. The myth started that ostriches bury their heads in the sand. Thousands of years later, many people still believe it to be true. Ostriches sometimes move

From afar, it can look like ostriches are putting their heads on or in the ground.

43

Speed, in miles per hour (70 km/h), an ostrich can run.

- Ostriches do not bury their heads.
- They bring their heads close to the ground to make nests, tend their eggs, and search for food.
- Ostriches hide by blending into the landscape.

Ostriches keep their heads at ground level when checking on eggs.

their heads close to the ground. It looks like their heads are in the sand. What are these African birds actually doing?

Modern scientists know ostriches lower their heads to the ground for several reasons. The birds dig large, shallow nests in the ground. They use their beaks to turn their eggs many times each day. Ostriches also eat plants along the ground. They reach down to swallow sand and pebbles. This helps grind up their food. Ostriches have huge bodies and small heads. From a distance, it may look like they are

sticking their heads in the sand.

When they see a predator, ostriches may try to hide. But they grow up to 9 feet (2.7 m) tall. They have few places to hide on the plains of Africa. Instead, they lie flat on the ground with their necks pressed down. Their bodies look like rocks or shrubs. Their black-and-white coloring helps them blend in. But their heads stay out of the sand.

Busted: Camels Store Water in Their Humps

Camels are hardy mammals that live in deserts. They can withstand conditions that would kill many other animals. Camels survive extreme temperatures with very little food or water.

Scientists have studied how camels survive desert life. Camels have two rows of long eyelashes. These protect their eyes from sand. Camels' nostrils can close. This keeps moisture in and sand out. They drink gallons of water at a time. Many people assume the camel's hump stores extra water.

But a camel's hump does not hold any water at all. Camel humps are full of fat. This fat is a

FLOPPY HUMPS

When a camel is well fed, its hump is plump. But that changes if the animal goes for a long time without food. The camel will use the fat in its hump for fuel. The hump loses its shape as fat is used up. A used-up hump will be droopy and limp. Once the camel rests and eats, its hump will plump back up.

20
Gallons (76 L) of water a camel can drink at one time.

- Many people assume a camel's hump is filled with water, but it is actually filled with fat.
- Scientists used to think the fat in a camel's hump could turn into water, but this is not true.
- A camel's blood cells store extra water.

source of energy when there is no food. Storing fat in a pile on top is an advantage. Storing fat around the body would make a camel too hot. A camel's hump also shields the rest of the animal from the sun.

Scientists used to think this fat could be changed into water. But this theory was incorrect. Instead, camels store extra water in their blood. They have special blood cells. These cells can grow to almost 2.5 times their normal size. This allows them to store extra

water. The cells are shaped like ovals rather than circles. Their shape allows the cells to flow more freely. A camel's hump is a storage tank. But it is full of fat, not water.

Camel humps store fat, not water.

Busted:
Bats Are Blind

The Spanish word for *bat* means "blind mouse." English speakers have the expression "blind as a bat." The idea that bats are blind is a myth. But how they are able to fly swiftly and accurately in the dark was a long-standing mystery. Scientists worked for more than two centuries to find out how bats did it.

In 1790, an Italian scientist studied how bats hunt. Lazzaro Spallanzani put blinded bats through an obstacle course. Even without vision, the bats were capable fliers. Then,

he plugged the bats' ears. The bats started to run into obstacles. Spallanzani knew something in the ear was crucial to a bat's ability to fly. But he did not know what or how.

More than a century later, scientists Donald Griffin and Robert Galambos conducted a study. In 1938, they found bats use something called echolocation to guide them. They make high-pitched sounds and listen for the echoes. The echoes tell them where their prey is. When Spallanzani plugged the bats' ears,

Despite popular belief, bats have good eyesight.

he made it impossible for the bats to hear the echoes.

It does not seem like bats need to see. But all bats can. Recent research shows bats use both vision and echolocation when they hunt. Their eyes help them keep track of where they are going. Echolocation helps them find small, moving insects that would be hard to see. Using both, bats can find very small targets.

Some bigger bats have very large eyes and excellent vision. Fruit-eating bats use their big eyes to find flowers and fruit in the dark. But big or small, bats are not blind.

Vampire bats feed off the blood of large mammals, including livestock.

0
Number of the 1,100 bat species worldwide that are blind.

- Because bats hunt in the dark, people mistake them for being blind.
- All bat species can see, and many see very well.
- Bats use their vision and echolocation to help them find prey.

VAMPIRE BATS

Vampire bats are the only mammals that feed solely on blood from other mammals. They use their excellent eyesight to find prey. They can spot another mammal from hundreds of feet away. They use razor-sharp teeth to bite sleeping horses and cattle. Then, the bats drink the blood. Bats do not take enough blood to cause harm. But cuts from the bats can become infected. They rarely bite humans.

Busted: Sheep Are Not Very Bright

In 2006, 450 sheep in Eastern Turkey plunged to their deaths. In another instance, one sheep tried to cross a deep ravine. It fell. The others followed and fell, too. Observations like these ones led scientists to assume sheep are stupid.

Sheep are highly domesticated. Humans have bred them to have a strong instinct to follow their flock. This makes sheep easier to care for in large numbers. Being part of a flock protects sheep against predators. But it can also get them into trouble.

A 2001 scientific study found sheep are smarter than people assume. British researchers Jennifer Morton and Laura Avanzo were studying a human brain disease. They performed tests on genetically modified sheep. These sheep had the same defective gene that causes a brain disease in humans. Despite the gene, the sheep in the study recognized dozens of different sheep faces. They remembered these faces for more than two years.

Sheep are herd animals that stay with their flocks.

Sheep are very good at remembering their surroundings. Other researchers set up a maze. Sheep had to get through it to get to their flock. The more practice the sheep had, the faster they got through the maze.

Recent studies show sick sheep will eat certain plants that can help them feel better. Dr. Dean Revell is a scientist who studies sheep nutrition. His research finds that lambs learn from their mothers how to find medicinal plants.

50
Number of faces sheep recognized in a 2001 study.

- Sheep have a strong instinct to stay with their flock, which may get them into trouble.
- Sheep can recognize many of the other sheep in their flock.
- They can learn and remember mazes and find medicinal plants.

Sheep recognize the faces of their flockmates.

Busted: Chameleons Change Color to Blend In

Chameleons are lizards found in Madagascar, Africa, the Middle East, and southern Europe. They can change color. Most change from brown to green. Some display shades of pink, blue, orange, red, yellow, green, purple, and turquoise.

Since the 1960s, scientists have studied why chameleons change color. They used to think chameleons change color to hide from predators. But recently, scientists have discovered the opposite is true. Chameleons change color to stand out. They often exchange their resting colors of green or brown for bright colors. They do it so other chameleons notice them. It is a way to communicate.

Scientists used to think chameleons change color to blend in.

> Now, scientists know chameleons change color to communicate.

Scientists have found that different colors on different body parts have specific meanings. Males use bright colors to attract mates. Females use bright colors to reject them. Bright colors also show when a chameleon is willing to fight. Greys and browns mean a chameleon does not want any trouble. Chameleons use their amazing ability to change color to express themselves. They do not change color to blend in.

THINK ABOUT IT

What are some other ways animals communicate with each other? What are some of the messages they might send to members of the same species? To animals that are different?

20
Seconds it takes a chameleon to change color.

- Chameleons are usually green or brown.
- They change color to attract attention, not to hide.
- They display bright color patterns to communicate with other chameleons.

Busted: Porcupines Shoot Their Quills

The myth that porcupines shoot quills has ancient origins. Ancient Greek philosophers Aristotle, Pliny, and Aelian all mentioned this belief in their writing on natural history. Porcupines are nearsighted and move slowly. They protect themselves with spines called quills. These special, hard hairs have sharp tips. They grow all over the porcupine. Only the porcupine's stomach has no quills.

Porcupines cannot shoot their quills. But there may be times when it seems like they do. Scientists have observed how porcupines act around predators. First, porcupines give warning signals. Their quills go from lying flat to sticking out. They make clacking sounds. They also release a strong odor.

If the predator does not leave, the porcupine may jump or swing its tail at it. Quills that touch the predator fall off the porcupine. They stick firmly

Porcupines are intimidating-looking mammals.

into the predator. This happens very quickly. It can look like the porcupine shot its quills.

In 2012, researchers found that porcupine quills can stick into skin more easily than a needle can. The quills end in tiny barbs that make them difficult to remove. They cause painful wounds. If they reach organs, they can cause death. Porcupines grow new quills to replace those they lose.

Porcupines are not aggressive animals. They attack only if threatened. Even then, they are not able to shoot their quills.

Porcupines can regrow their quills.

30,000
**Number of quills
a porcupine has
on its body.**

- A porcupine will puff out its quills when it feels threatened.
- If a predator will not leave it alone, the porcupine may jump at it.
- The quills fall off the porcupine and stick into the predator.

Busted: Snakes Unhinge Their Jaws to Swallow Prey

Snakes can swallow prey bigger than their heads. They can open their mouths very wide. Their top and bottom jaws almost form a straight line. Many scientists and the public believe snakes unhinge their jaws while eating.

But that is not true. In reality, snakes' jaws stay connected, even when they are opened their widest.

The two halves of a human's lower jaw are fused together. A snake's are not. Each side can move separately from the other. They can also spread very far apart.

A human's upper and lower jaws join right below the ear. A snake has an extra bone where its jaws join. It is called the quadrate bone. This bone is very loosely attached to the

This rattlesnake's jaws open wide so it can swallow its prey whole.

Many snakes are eager eaters.

skull. It works together with stretchy tissues. This allows the snake's jaws more range of motion. They make a double hinge between the top and bottom jaws. This allows the snake's mouth to open wider. Snakes also have stretchy skin and muscles. All this helps them swallow their meals in one huge, very slow gulp.

100
Percent of its body size a snake can eat.

- Snakes cannot unhinge their jaws.
- Their lower front jaws are not attached at the center, making them very flexible.
- Snakes can swallow prey that is bigger than their heads.

GIANT APPETITES

Snakes have been known to swallow some giant meals. A Burmese python once swallowed a whole crocodile. If a meal is too big, it could rot before it is digested. Sometimes, snakes throw up the rotting animal. Other times, it can make the snake sick or even kill it.

Fact Sheet

- Sometimes experiments do not—or cannot—collect all the facts. For example, in early experiments, scientists used thermometers to take cheetahs' temperatures. Today, they can attach sensors to the cheetahs' bodies. They are more accurate than thermometers. Scientists now can measure cheetahs' temperatures no matter what they are doing.

- Scientists are not always right. John James Audubon was certain vultures could not smell. But the experiments he did had problems. He used very rotten meat that vultures do not like. He did not really consider the different kinds of vultures. We now know black vultures mostly use their eyes to find food. Turkey vultures mostly use odor.

- Sometimes books have false information in them. People may read something in a book and accept it as true, even if it is not. Pliny the Elder wrote 37 natural history books. Many of the things he wrote and believed to be true were not. His books may have started the myth about ostriches hiding their heads in the ground.

- One thing we know for sure is that animals are fascinating. People will continue to study and uncover the many mysteries of the animal kingdom.

Glossary

captive
Held or confined and not able to escape.

carcass
The dead body of an animal.

domesticated
Adapted to living with and being used by humans.

glands
Parts of the body that create a substance, such as sweat.

naturalist
A person who studies living things.

nearsighted
Able to see things clearly only if they are close.

ornithologist
A scientist who studies birds.

prey
An animal hunted or killed by another for food.

species
A category of related living things.

tissue
A group or layer of cells that form basic parts of the body.

For More Information

Books

1,000 Strange But True Animal Facts. Bath, UK: Parragon, 2014.

Jenkins, Steve. *The Animal Book: A Collection of the Fastest, Fiercest, Toughest, Cleverest, Shyest—and Most Surprising—Animals on Earth.* Boston: Houghton Mifflin Harcourt, 2013.

Wild Animal Atlas: Earth's Astonishing Animals and Where They Live. Washington, DC: National Geographic, 2010.

Visit 12StoryLibrary.com

Scan the code or use your school's login at **12StoryLibrary.com** for recent updates about this topic and a full digital version of this book. Enjoy free access to:

- Digital ebook
- Breaking news updates
- Live content feeds
- Videos, interactive maps, and graphics
- Additional web resources

Note to educators: Visit 12StoryLibrary.com/register to sign up for free premium website access. Enjoy live content plus a full digital version of every 12-Story Library book you own for every student at your school.

Index

Aelian, 24
Africa, 4, 15, 22
Aristotle, 24
Audubon, John James, 6–7
Australia, 8, 9
Avanzo, Laura, 20

bats, 18–19
black vultures, 6
blood sweat, 4–5
Burmese pythons, 27

camels, 16–17
chameleons, 22–23
Chapman, Frank, 6, 7
cheetahs, 12–13

de Blainwill, Henri, 8
dogs, 10–11

echolocation, 18–19
Europe, 22

Galambos, Robert, 18
germs, 5, 11
Griffin, Donald, 18

hippopotamus, 4–5

Japan, 5

koalas, 8–9

Madagascar, 22
Middle East, 22
Morton, Jennifer, 20

ostriches, 14–15

Pliny the Elder, 14, 24
porcupines, 24–25

Revell, Dean, 21

sheep, 20–21
snakes, 26–27
Spallanzani, Lazzaro, 18
Stager, Kenneth, 7

Turkey, 20
turkey vultures, 6–7

vampire bats, 19

About the Author

Jodie Mangor loves all sorts of animals. She lives in Ithaca, New York, where she edits scientific papers (many of them on animals) and writes for children.

READ MORE FROM 12-STORY LIBRARY

Every 12-Story Library book is available in many formats. For more information, visit 12StoryLibrary.com.